True Stories and Fascinating Facts

About the 1960s

A Fun Facts Book

Jonny Katz

Table of Contents

Introduction

The 1960s was a wild decade filled with political upheaval, civil rights activism, major advances in medicine and technology, and drastic changes in fashion and music.

Long hair, bell bottoms, and an increasing dissatisfaction with the status quo were the order of the day.

Television became an important part of family life. Daytime soaps got their start in the sixties. During prime time, the family could sit down and watch Star Trek, The Twilight Zone, or for lighter fare, Get Smart or The Dick Van Dyke Show.

The computer was becoming more and more important to daily lives with inventions such as the ATM and early programmable calculators.

This book is chock full of interesting bits of information about this fascinating time. Some of the names, trivia, stories and fascinating facts might be familiar to you. Others will take you by surprise.

Want More Fascinating Facts?

Get your free copy of
Now, That's Interesting
by Jonny Katz

Just drop us an email:
OldTownPublishing@gmail.com

Remembering the 1960s

In the News

The Dictator Who Refused to Die

Some people are really tough to kill.

According to a former head of Cuban intelligence, Fidel Castro survived at least 634 assassination attempts by the CIA. (Talk about feeling unwanted.)

I don't know how accurate that figure is, and it's probably an exaggeration, but I think we can safely assume Castro dodged the proverbial bullet hundreds of times and in many ways.

Here are just a few of the known bungled assassination plans and actual attempts against the Cuban dictator made over the decades by the CIA.

Exploding Cigar: Probably the most famous attempt on Castro's life was the exploding cigar idea concocted in 1961. The CIA spiked a box of cigars with a botulinum toxin strong enough to kill anyone who put one in his mouth. No one knows what happened to the cigars, but it became obvious they were never smoked by "El Comandante".

Hoping for a Psychedelic Speech

Hoping to undermine the dictator's public image, the CIA cooked up a plant to spray a broadcasting studio with a chemical similar in effect to LSD. The thought was to get the dictator to hallucinate on air. The US spy organization never figured out how to do this safely and gave up the plan.

The Diving Suit
In another 1961 assassination attempt, the CIA planned to have American hostage negotiator and lawyer James Donavan give Castro a diving

suit contaminated with skin-eating fungus and a tuberculosis infected breathing apparatus. The plan fell apart when Donavan, hearing about the plan and what the CIA wanted him to do, gave Fidel a different suit.

The Poisoned Pen

This CIA master plan involved rigging a pen with a tiny needle containing poison. An official close to Castro was offered the pen, but he felt the CIA could come up with something a little more sophisticated.

Look at the Pretty Seashell

Under the category of plans that were too stupid to even be attempted was the "painted seashell caper." In 1963 intelligence officials thought of hiding explosives inside a large, exotically painted sea shell. That idea was never tried and turned out to be another bomb.

Castro's Shoes

The CIA had apparently also planned to dust Castro's shoes with thallium salts in an attempt to make his beard fall out. No agent ever got close enough to Fidel's footwear to give this one a go.

In the end, Fidel Castro died quietly, in his bed, at the age of 90, on the evening of 25 November 2016. His body was cremated and his ashes interned in Santiago de Cuba.

A City Divided

At the end of World War II, Germany was divided into four Allied occupation zones, as was the German capital of Berlin. In 1948, the United States, Britain and France combined their three sectors into one – the Federal Republic of Germany, more commonly known as West Germany. The fourth zone, East Germany, remained with the Soviet Union.

Between 1949 and 1961, East Germans were becoming more and more dissatisfied living life in the communist system when, so close, was the democratic west. Germans began fleeing from East to West Germany at a rate of 2,000 per day. By 1961, about 2.5 million had crossed the border. Many of these people were skilled laborers, professionals, and intellectuals.

Rather than the logical approach – make the East a place where people want to live – Soviet leader

Nikita Khrushchev told East Germany to build a wall.

In one night, August 12-13, 1961, over 30 miles of barbed wire were strung through the heart of Berlin. On August 15th, the building of the infamous wall began in earnest. The wall continued to grow and expand, including an additional 850-mile construction outside of Berlin.

With the border sealed, the escape attempts from the Soviet controlled East began. During the construction of the wall, one young East German soldier, Konrad Schumann, became a symbol of the desire for freedom when, while no other soldiers were watching, he removed some of the fortification, dropped his machine gun, and jumped over the wall, running to sanctuary in the West. West German photographer Peter Leibing photographed his escape. The photograph, later title "Leap into

Freedom" became an iconic image of the Cold War.

Escape attempts continued throughout the years until the wall was brought down in 1990. When the wall fell, the East and West were formally reunited into one country.

One Giant Leap for Mankind

In 1961, President John F. Kennedy delivered a speech to a special joint session of congress. In it he offered this challenge to NASA and to America, "I believe that this nation should commit itself to achieving the goal, before this decade is out, of landing a man on the moon and returning him safely to earth."

At the time of the President's speech, the United States was trailing the Soviet Union in "the space race". The U.S. needed a singularly huge achievement to outstrip the Soviets of their position as number one in space exploration.

On July 20th, 1969, with the landing of Apollo 11s lunar module *Eagle* in the Sea of Tranquility,

NASA fulfilled that goal set by President Kennedy.

Over half a billion people around the world held their breath as American astronaut Neil Armstrong descended from the lunar module, stepped off the ladder and placed his foot firmly upon the powdery surface of the moon. Here he spoke his famous line *"that's one small step for a man, one giant leap for mankind."*

Buzz Aldrin joined him 19 minutes later. They performed a few scientific tests, took photographs, packed up soil and rock samples, and planted the U.S. Flag. A few hours later, both men were back in the *Eagle.* At 5:35 p.m. on the 21st, Buzz Aldrin and Neil Armstrong rejoined their fellow astronaut pilot Michael Collins in the Command Module and Apollo 11 headed home, safely splashing down in the Pacific Ocean on July 24th.

Among the items left behind to mark the historic moment was a plaque signed by the three crew members and the President of the United States, "Here men from the planet Earth first set foot upon the Moon, July 1969 A.D. We came in peace for all mankind."

Martin Luther King Jr. Has a Dream

The face and name most associated with the American Civil Rights movement is Martin Luther King Jr.

This great man was a charismatic leader, social activist, and Baptist Minister. He earned his doctorate in systematic theology in 1953.

In 1954, while living in Montgomery, Alabama, the center of the Civil Rights movement, Martin Luther King became the official leader of the Montgomery Bus Boycott.

King was heavily influenced by Mahatma Gandhi, and was dedicated to achieving full equality for the African American through civil disobedience and non-violent protest.

In November 1956, when the Supreme Court ruled, finding segregation on buses unconstitutional, King was already in the spotlight, leading the way in non-violent civil rights activism.

Frequently the target of white supremacists, Martin Luther King's Montgomery home was firebombed and in 1958, while at a book signing in a Harlem bookstore, he was stabbed in the chest. The attack reinforced his resolve to create social change through non-violent means.

On 28 August 1963, in one of the most historically significant moments of the 1960s, Martin Luther King Jr. stood on the steps of the Lincoln Memorial in front of 250,000 people and gave his eloquent and powerful "I Have a Dream Speech".

That speech, part of the historic *March on Washington*, would mark the turning point for the American Civil Rights movement.

From 1957 to 1968, he spoke at over 2500 events and traveled over six million miles.

On October 14th, 1964, King received the Nobel Peace Prize for the non-violent combating of racial inequality.

Martin Luther King Jr. continue to lead and inspire the civil rights movement until his assassination on April 4th 1968.

A monument dedicated to King stands on the National Mall in Washington D.C.
Martin Luther King Jr. is the only non-president to have a national holiday dedicated to his memory.

Among his most famous quotes is this; *"In the end, we will remember not the words of our enemies, but the silence of our friends."*

"He Was a Friend of Mine"

The 1960s saw both the election and the assassination of one of America's most beloved presidents. John Fitzgerald Kennedy was elected to office in November 1960 at the comparatively young age of 43, beating Richard Nixon by one of the narrowest margins in U.S. history.

Kennedy was astoundingly popular with an average job approval rating of 70%. (The average popularity rating for an American president while in office is 54%)

The president's biggest mistake was the embarrassing attempt to overthrow Fidel Castro in the catastrophic Bay of Pigs fiasco.

However, he is also hailed as a hero by Americans for his handling of the Cuban Missile

Crisis – quite possibly averting a nuclear war with the Soviet Union.

Here are just some of John F. Kennedy's achievements during his tenure as President of the United States:

He established the peace corps in 1961.
He took the U.S. economy out of recession through his reforms.

He established the *New Frontier,* a multifaceted domestic program aimed at improving the living standards of U.S. Citizens.

He contributed to the formation of the partial nuclear test ban treaty.

Kennedy strengthened the American Space Program.

He initiated the alliance for progress for development of Latin America – to establish cooperation between U.S. and countries south of her border.

He worked towards civil rights for African Americans.

He was responsible for the equal pay act of 1963, which abolished wage disparity based on sex.

The world wept when John F. Kennedy was assassinated on that cold Friday in November 1963. And a generation of Americans would remember exactly where they were when they heard that awful news.

When his body lay in state at the Capitol Rotunda, 250,000 people came to pay their respects.

His passing has been memorialized in many ways, including in these songs which invoke his memory:

"He Was a Friend of Mine" - The Byrds
"Abraham, Martin, and John" - Richard Holler / Dion
"The Day John Kennedy Died" – Lou Reed
"Sleeping In" – The Postal Service
"Life in a Northern Town" – Dream Academy
"Born in the 50s" – The Police
"Public Enemy #1" – Eminem
"Six White Horses" - Tommy Cash
"Civil War" – Guns N' Roses (1990)

"Let us not seek the Republican answer or the Democratic answer, but the right answer. Let us not seek to fix the blame for the past. Let us accept our own responsibility for the future." John F. Kennedy

Science, Medicine, and Technology

The Invention That Replaced Steel and Saved Lives

 Stephanie Kwolek, the daughter of two Polish immigrants, was a chemist working for the DuPont corporation in 1965 when she discovered a stronger-than-steel compound that would prove to be the strongest, stiffest fiber known.

That fiber, five times stronger than an equal weight of steel and lighter than fiberglass, came to be known as Kevlar - likely an invented word with no etymology (The company just made it up.)

DuPont had been searching for a fiber that was rigid, light, and strong to replace the steel wires used at that time in cars. The company could see the gasoline shortage looming in the near future and wanted to provide a stronger, lighter material for tires to help improve gas mileage.

As it turned out, Kwolek had discovered that, and much, much more. Kevlar bulletproof vests and body armor have saved the lives of thousands of service members and law enforcement officers over the last many decades. Her discovery is also used in boots to protect the feet of firefighters and in gloves to protect fingers of cooks and chefs from accidental cuts from cooking knives. The material is also used in ropes, bicycle tires, racing sales, and spacecraft components.

For twenty years following her discovery, Stephanie Kwolek continued to work at DuPont as the head of polymer research at its pioneering lab.

During her 40 years as a research scientist, Kwolek would earn 28 patents (including the one for Kevlar) and in 1995, Stephanie Kwolek was inducted into the National Inventors Hall of Fame.

Machines Don't Keep Bankers' Hours

Perhaps you don't remember leaving work early or foregoing a meal during your lunch break in order to run down and stand in line at the bank to make a deposit or get out cash. And forget entering those hallowed halls after 5pm, weekends, or any (and I mean *any* holiday).

That world began to change in June 1967 when the first ATM opened outside a branch of Barclays Bank in the Enfield area of London. People came from all around to watch as the first person placed a special check, encoded with carbon-14, into the machine, put in his PIN, and then a special plastic card and miraculously cash came out of a small metal slot. (This system for using an ATM has, obviously, been simplified over the years.)

The mastermind behind the ATM was John Shepherd-Barron, an Indian-born British inventor. Apparently, the idea came to him one day when he got to his bank one minute late and had to wait until the next day to withdraw the cash he needed. He put that problem together with the design of a chocolate vending machine. What if you could create a vending machine that would dispense cash?

I'm sure when that first automated teller machine was installed outside Barclays Bank in 1967, no one, not even its inventor, could see that it was a step toward the world of online commerce and digital currency of our current age.

Have a Heart

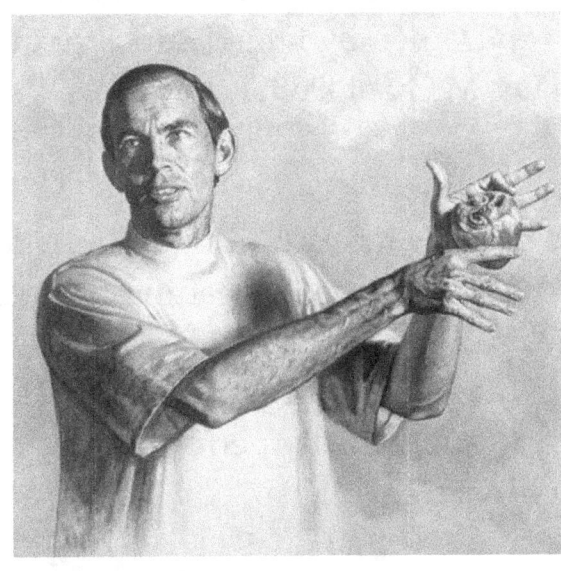

Huge strides were made in heart surgery during the 1960s.

The first successful human-to-human heart transplant was performed on December 3rd, 1967. A team of South African surgeons, led by Dr. Christian Barnard, transplanted the heart of Denise Darvall, a young accident victim, into the body of 54-year-old Louis Washkansky. The recipient died eighteen days later of pneumonia.

However, Dr. Barnard and his team performed a heart transplant on a second recipient, Philip Blaiberg, in 1968. The patient was able to leave the hospital and lived for another year and a half.

In May 1968, a brilliant Texas surgeon and surgical pioneer by the name of Dr. Denton

Cooley performed the first successful human to human heart transplant in the United States. Dr. Denton had been trained by famed educator and heart surgeon Dr. Michael DeBakey.

In his long and productive career, Cooley performed the world's first surgical implantation of an artificial heart. He was the leading pioneer in repairing heart defects in children, developed techniques for "bloodless" surgery, and was among the first to successfully perform a coronary artery bypass.

In addition to all his other "miracle" surgical developments and techniques, Dr. Cooley's early use of the heart and lung machine made open-heart surgery possible. He and his team at the Texas Heart Institute performed more than 100,000 open-heart surgeries over several decades.

During a trial later in his career, Cooley was asked by a lawyer if he thought he was the greatest heart surgeon in the world. Cooley replied simply, "yes".

"Don't you think that is being rather immodest?" the lawyer asked. "Perhaps," he replied. "But remember, I am under oath."

Dr. Denton Cooley was awarded the Medal of Freedom in 1984, the National Medal of Technology, and The Rene Leriche Prize – the highest honor of the International Surgical Society.

No Measly Discovery

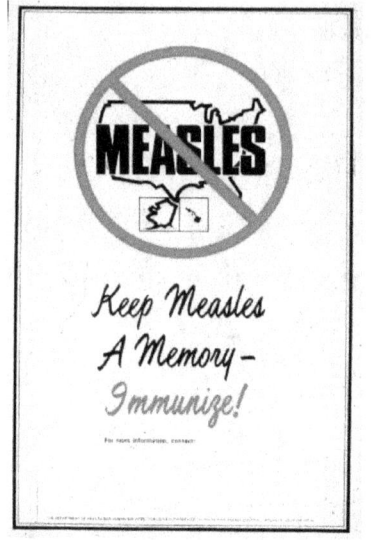

Keep Measles
A Memory –
Immunize!

By the time a measles vaccine was developed in the 1960s, the disease had been around and documented for over a thousand years.

One of the first cases was reported by a Persian doctor in the 9th century. In the middle of the 1700ds, Scottish physician Francis Home discovered the disease was caused by an infection found in the blood – but no prevention or cure could be found.

By 1912, measles had made its way to the shores of the United States. In the first decade of its appearance, the disease accounted for an average of 6,000 deaths per year. One out of every four thousand children who contracted the disease would suffer from swelling of the brain and end up mentally challenged. Mothers contracting the disease would frequently miscarry or give birth to children with severe physical defects.

Measles continued to sicken and kill people in America and around the world until, in 1954, two physicians in Boston, Massachusetts, finally isolated the measles virus and came up with a vaccine.

Virologist John F. Enders and fellow-scientist Thomas C. Peebles collected the blood from students who had become ill with measles, identifying and isolating the virus in the blood of a 13-year-old-boy named David Edmonston.

By 1963, the scientists at Harvard had developed a safe, and incredibly effective measles vaccine. An improved vaccine was developed by Maurice Hilleman and colleagues in 1968. They named it the Edmonston-Enders strain. This is the vaccine still in use today.

Almost immediately following the release of the vaccine, an all-out inoculation campaign began. The number of reported measles cases began to fall dramatically and by the year 2000, Measles was declared eliminated in the United States.

Global Warming Warning

By the 1960s, concern was increasing about the effects of human-caused pollution on the environment. It was a time of growing consciousness and feeling of responsibility toward the future of the quality of life on the planet.

The bestselling book *Silent Spring*, written by American biologist, Rachel Carson, was published in 1962. Her warnings on the horrific effects of DDT and other pesticides on the environment opened the eyes of her thousands of readers to the potential dangers of pollution. This book is acclaimed as the most influential and far-reaching writing about environmental concerns ever published.

The term "greenhouse gasses" became part of American culture in the 1960s as people became more aware of the effects of air pollution from the burning of fossil fuels such as coal and oil, including the emissions from the growing number of cars.

Studies began that would result in environmental protection laws and ultimately the creation of the Environmental Protection Agency by President Richard Nixon in December 1970.

A lesser-known story involves a French plan to dump atomic waste into the Mediterranean Sea. It took the combined efforts of Jacques Cousteau and Prince Rainier III of Monaco averted this catastrophe.

In 1969, inspired by the Civil Rights Movement, Democrat Gaylord Nelson and Republican congressman Pete McCloskey started an educational "teach-in" movement that would, in 1970, become known as *Earth Day*.

The concerted effort that began in earnest during this decade brought about far-reaching changes in the outlook of society toward the effects of human activity on the earth.

Sports

Overtaking the Sultan of Swat

In 1927, in a race that rivetted the attention of baseball fans across the United States, New York Yankee star Babe Ruth and a young upstart Yankee named Lou Gehrig became locked in a battle for the most single-season home runs.

In a record that would stand for 34 years, Babe Ruth won that race with an astounding 60 homers to Gehrig's 47.

However, in 1961, another home run race would grab the attention of baseball fans. This was the year that pitted another two New York Yankees against one-another for the title of *home run king*.

Mickey Mantle had been a Bronx Bomber for a decade and New York fans loved him. Competing against him was a relative newcomer, Roger Maris.

Mantle and Maris both hit home run after home run during that famous 1961 season. This battle for home run greatness became the talk of the season, not only among Yankee fans, but among baseball fans across the country.

Then, on October 1st, at exactly 2:43 in the afternoon, while President John F. Kennedy was telling the world about America's goal to land on the moon, another heavenly sphere rose over the fences deep in center field. In the last game of the 1961 season, Roger Maris broke one of the most hallowed records in baseball. His 61 home runs beat Babe Ruth's record by 1. When the season was over, Mickey Mantle had hit just 54.

That 1961 New York Yankees team went all the way to winning the World Series and is often cited unofficially as the best baseball team of all time.

"Float Like a Butterfly, Sting Like a Bee"

One of the most dramatic moments in sports history happened on 25 Feb, 1964. That was the date Cassius Clay would challenge the dominating Sonny Liston for the title of Heavyweight Champion of the World.

It was supposed to be a one-sided fight, a huge mismatch, a thrashing of the 22-year-old Clay by current boxing veteran and champion Sonny Liston.

Liston was a 1-8 favorite. Not only did he come into the fight with an impressive 35-1 record, but he emanated menace. After all, he learned how to box while in the Missouri State Penitentiary, while doing time for armed robbery and was said to be linked to organized crime. His last three fights had ended in first round knockouts.

Cassius Clay seemed ill-suited to participate against such a powerful opponent. His last two fights were a disputed 10-round decision and a fifth round TKO.

But Cassius Clay and his trainer Angelo Dundee had studied film of his opponent. – looking for flaws and any way he telegraphed his punches. He also enjoyed a bit of psychological warfare insulting the champion and reciting annoying poems and rhymes.

When the fighters entered the ring, no one realistically thought Cassius Clay had a chance against the champion. The Convention Hall was half full, with only slightly more than 8,000 fans arriving to watch the show. Most Americans, interested in the sport, would hear the call on the radio with Les Keiter and Howard Cosell.

The fight went back and forth, with Cassius Clay showing his amazing power, speed and skill. Clay took over in the 6th round, pummeling Liston with blow after blow to the champion's already puffy face.

After the sixth round, Sonny Liston remained on his stool and never came out for the seventh.

In the biggest upset in the history of boxing, Cassius Clay – the man who would later become Muhammed Ali - became the youngest heavyweight champion in history.

Sidewalk Surfing

The earliest skateboards made from planks of wood and roller skate wheels were first built over a hundred years ago, around the turn of the 20th century.

However, it was in the early 1960s that the sport of skateboarding really took off. When the waves weren't cooperating and regular ocean surfing wasn't an available option, kids turned to *sidewalk surfing.*

In 1963, two skateboard manufacturers, Makaha and Hobie, seeing the rising popularity of the sport, began promoting skateboarding with professional teams and competitions. The first such competition was held in Hermosa Beach, California. Events included the downhill slalom and the freestyle skate.

Surfing, skateboarding and fun in the sun became a dream life captured in movies, television and song.

The popularity of sidewalk surfing continued throughout the 1960s. In 1964 *Jan and Dean* recorded "Sidewalk Surfin" which rose to number 25 on Billboard's Hot 100. Also in 1964, the duo did a skateboard demonstration for Dick Clark on American Bandstand.

When safety concerns began to grow and skateboarding became less accepted, the sport developed its own underground language and culture. Then, with the advent of the X Games and popularity of extreme sports in the 1990s, sidewalk surfing moved back into the mainstream.

In the summer of 2020, when it made its Olympic Games debut in Tokyo, skateboarding became an official extreme sport.

A One Woman Track and Field Show

Wilma Rudolph was an American athletic phenom. As a child, she had overcome a multitude of illnesses, including a case of polio, which left her wearing a leg brace until the age of twelve.

She was still a sophomore at Tennessee State when she set a new world record in the 200-meter dash – a record that would stand for eight years. She also qualified as a member of the running team for the 1960 Summer Olympics. (Wilma is on the far left in this photo of the Olympic relay team)

At those Olympics held in Rome, Italy, Wilma Rudolph competed in three track events. She won her first Gold in the 100-meter dash and three days later, took the Gold in the 200-meter, after setting a new Olympic record in the opening heat.

Then came the race she wanted to win more than any other – the 4X100 meter relay. She had beaten her teammates in the first two races and wanted them to also take home a gold medal.

On September 8th, 1960 with her team, made up entirely of Tennessee State Tigerbelles, Wilma Rudolph won her third gold of the VXII Olympiad.

Rudolph became the first American woman to win three gold medals in a single Olympic Games.

After her record-breaking speeds and triple-gold performance, Wilma became known around the world as "the fastest woman in history". A woman of charm, humor, humanity and fierce determination, Rudolph became an international star.

Her legacy lives on, inspiring young athletes of a new generation.

In 1984, the Women's Sports Foundation named Rudolph one of the five greatest American women athletes.

Wilma Rudolph is included in many halls of fame including:

Black Sports Hall of Fame
National Women's Hall of Fame
U.S. Olympics Hall of Fame
U.S. National Track and Field Hall of Fame

Bill Mazeroski Walks Off

In the 7th and final game of the 1960 World Series, fans were treated to two of the most tense and exciting innings in the history of baseball.

The Pittsburgh Pirates were viewed as underdogs to the mighty New York Yankees. The Pirates had already shown their resilience by winning the National League Pennant seven games ahead of the second-place Milwaukee Braves. Now, they had lasted to take the World Series into a 7th game.

The Bronx Bombers had outscored Pittsburgh 46-17 in the first 6 games of the series.

After taking back the lead from the Yankees, the Pirates were leading 9-7 in the top of the ninth and needed just three outs to win. Pirates reliever Bob Friend was replaced by Harvey Haddix after relinquishing two consecutive singles. He got Roger Maris to pop up, but then Mickey Mantle hit a run-scoring single and Yogi

Berra followed with a fielder's choice. The Yankees had tied the game.

In the bottom of the ninth inning, the first Pirates batter to step to the place was a future Hall of Famer known more for his glove than his bat. Mazeroski had hit just 11 home runs in the entire season. But Bill Mazeroski was about to pick up his bat and make history, entering forever into baseball lore.

Mazeroski took the Yankee pitcher's second offering for the ride of its life, sending it over the 406-foot marker in left-center field. Yogi Berra and Mickey Mantle could only watch as the baseball sailed over the ivy-covered brick wall of Forbes Field and into the green foliage of the park beyond.

The stunned Yankees walked off the field. Bill Mazeroski and the Pirates celebrated Pittsburgh's first World Series title in 35 years, while baseball fans celebrated what has become known as the most exciting game in the history of the World Series.

Popular Culture

It's a Small World After All

The Disney *It's a Small World* ride with its all-too-catchy song was originally created for the UNICEF Pavilion at the 1964 World's Fair in New York.

Due to disagreements which had to be ironed out with Pepsi, the sponsor of the ride, Disney Imagineers had only 11 months in which to come up with the concept and get an okay from the board. The plans met with full-hearted approval.

The ride itself was designed and constructed at Disney facilities in Burbank, California, and carefully shipped across country and put together in its temporary home in New York.

With the world moving at breakneck speed, it seems the public were more than ready for an uplifting ride with an inspiring theme (not to mention the simple but truly memorable theme song). People of all ages enjoyed the experience and thousands, eventually millions of dollars, would be donated to UNICEF as a result of *It's a Small World*. (At this writing, Disney continues to support UNICEF and their programs to help children around the world.)

Among other achievements, the ride was one of the first of its kind to be able to efficiently manage a continuous stream of guests, while letting each group enjoy the experience individually.

After the World's Fair, *It's a Small World* returned to its permanent home in Anaheim, California at Disneyland where it has been enjoyed by tens of thousands of visitors – many of whom probably still can't get that darned song out of their minds.

Julia Child Brings French Cooking to America

Before Graham Kerr, The Galloping Gourmet; before Gordon Ramsey, Rachel Ray or Anthony Bourdin there was the wonderful, unique, charming (and tall) Julia Child.

In 1961, the face of culinary America and palates of Americans were changed forever with the publication of *Mastering the Art of French Cooking* by Julia Child with her co-authors Louisette Bertholle and Simone Beck. That now-legendary cookbook received an overwhelmingly positive reception and ultimately helped launched Julia Child's television career.

It was in her first appearance on television in 1962 that viewers first got a glimpse of Julia Child. She was featured on a National Educational Television book review program. Instead of discussing her newly released cookbook, Julia showed the host and audience at home how to cook an omelet. Viewers loved her.

She was given her own show, which had its debut in February, 1963. With her warmth, enthusiasm, and humor, as well as an immense amount of technical skill, Julia and her show, *The French Chef* were an immediate success. The show ran for ten years, winning Peabody and Emmy Awards during that time. Julia became a cultural icon.

Child inspired millions of readers and viewers to have fun cooking and to appreciate the simple pleasure of food.

Julia Child was awarded the "James Beard Award for Chefs and Restaurants and the Primetime Emmy for Achievements in Educational Television. She has received honorary doctorates from several universities, including Harvard, Smith, and Brown.

In 2003, she was presented with the Medal of Freedom, the highest civilian award in the United States.

Today, Julia's enthusiasm and love of food are carried on in the charitable foundation she created in 1995. *The Julia Child Foundation for Gastronomy and Culinary Arts* offers grants to support gastronomical and culinary endeavors.

Movie-Goers Say YES to "Dr. No"

The first cinema-released James Bond movie, *Dr. No*, was released to theaters in 1962. The film received mixed reviews, but the public (frequently smarter than movie critics) loved it – as was proved by box office receipts.

Dr. No introduced much of the humor, class, gadgetry, beautiful locales, inventive methods of execution, intimations of sex, and unbounding action we now expect from a James Bond film.

You have the uber-evil villain - the Chinese-German criminal scientist with prosthetic metal hands, Dr. Julius No

A large and complicated evil scheme – Disrupt *Project Mercury* space launch at Cape Canaveral.

Exotic locations - Jamaica, Crab Key, and a mythical island off the coast of Jamaica.

Inventive ways of attempting to kill Bond - a tarantula, a flame-thrower disguised as a dragon, and a swamp contaminated with radiation.

A beautiful woman – Honey Ryder, played by Ursula Andress

And, of course, there was the man with a "license to kill", James Bond 007, portrayed by the suave and handsome Sean Connery.

Although many other actors played the role after him, Connery was the man who did more than any other to establish the character of 007. His elegant, sophisticated style and dry wit would become the hallmarks of James Bond throughout the following 27 films.

James Bond is a character created by British spy writer Ian Fleming and the movies are based on his books.

Albert Broccoli and Harry Saltzman purchased the movie rights to the series in 1961 and were the geniuses behind the classic feel and look that made James Bond films the special experience that they were - from the opening credits, theme music, and featured song all the way through to the close with Bond and his beautiful co-star disobeying orders as they enjoy each other's company.

"Next Stop, The Twilight Zone"

The interest in science fiction that began in the 1950s flourished during the following decade.

No more was this evident than in the number of television shows centering on futuristic themes of rocket ships, robots, and space travel. From The Jetsons to Star Trek; from Johnny Quest to My Favorite Martian and Dr. Who viewers of all ages could sit in front of their screens and be taken to another time or another planet.

For fantasy and horror, you could always turn to ABC on Monday nights and tune in to *The Outer Limits*.

However, although Star Trek could take you "where no man as gone before" only one show could take you to another dimension.

That show was The Twilight Zone. The introduction to every episode, told to the audience by Rod Serling, the show's creator, is always along these lines, "You're traveling through another dimension, a dimension not only of sight and sound but of mind. A journey into a wondrous land of imagination. Next stop, the Twilight zone!".

The Twilight Zone aired its first episode in October 1959 and continued until June 1964. It aired once a week and won numerous awards, including three Emmy Awards and a Golden Globe. In total 156 episodes were broadcast in those five seasons – many of these remain classics to this day.

Masterful writing, great acting and directing, and a completely untethered imagination made The Twilight Zone the best of the best science fiction horror genre television shows of its time.

The United States Says "Zip It"

All of us have written a zip code at the end of an address on a letter or package. And maybe, if we thought about it at all, we assumed the "zip" in zip code was there to mean something on the order of "move along quickly". If you thought that, you're partly correct.

The "ZIP" in ZIP code is an acronym for Zone Improvement Plan and was indeed chosen to suggest adding the code at the end of the address would make the mail reach its destination more quickly and efficiently.

The United States Postal Service introduced the ZIP code in its basic 5-digit format in 1963 to aid in the delivery of mail to a constantly growing populace.

Numerical postal codes in the United States began in 1943 when the USPS began adding a 2-digit code designating a postal district/zone predominantly in larger cities.

For example, in 1950, an address might look like this:
Joe Jones
1123 Main Street
San Francisco 15, California

In 1963, that address might look like:
Joe Jones
1123 Main Street
San Francisco, CA 94115

The first number in the ZIP code represents the state. The second and third digits stand for a large, local postal distribution facility, the fourth and fifth represent the part of the city, town or rural area.

In 1967, the post office used a cartoon character called Mr. Zip to promote the importance of using ZIP codes

With the increase in U.S. population over the years, it became necessary to add even more numbers to the end of an address. In 1983, the Postal Service introduced the +4 expanded ZIP code system we use today.

This And That About the 1960s

Innovator and engineer Douglas Engelbart of Stanford Research Center invented the computer mouse in 1963. The first of these devices was carved out of wood and had two wheels mounted on the bottom instead of the ball found in later computer mouses or the flat surface of current ones. Before coming up with the mouse design, Engelbart and fellow scientists had tried a host of other concepts including a foot pedal and a head-mounted apparatus.

Starting in 1966, health warnings began to be printed on cigarette packages.

In October 1962, Johnny Carson took over from Jack Paar as host of the Tonight Show. Carson ruled the late-night airwaves for 30 years.

John F. Kennedy established the Peace Corps by executive order in March, 1961. This development assistance program was authorized by Congress the following September. At its peak in 1966, the organization included 15,556 volunteers in 52 countries.

During the 1960s, the Vietnam War continued to escalate and opposition to the conflict mounted and anti-Vietnam protests became more common.

On the commercial side of popular culture, Sam Walton opened the very first Walmart in Rogers, Arkansas, in 1962. The retail chain, which is still owned by the Walton family, is one of the largest corporations in the world today.

The first three stars on Hollywood's Walk of Fame were John Wayne, Joanne Woodward, and Stanley Kramer, all placed in early 1960.

In 1963, Sidney Poitier won the Academy Award for "Best Actor" for his role as a construction worker who helps build a chapel in *Lilies of the*

Field. He became the first black actor to win the Best Actor Oscar. (Hattie McDaniel was the first Black performer to win an Academy Award. She earned the trophy for Best Supporting Actress for her portrayal of Mammy in *Gone with the Wind*. The movie came out in 1939 and in 1940 Hattie McDaniel had to accept her award in a segregated hotel.)

The first Target opened in 1960 with free parking, air conditioning, discount prices, and self-service shopping.

Slogan buttons first began in 1896, during the presidential race between McKinley and Bryan. But in the 1960s, displaying buttons on jackets, book covers, purses, and backpacks became a craze. The buttons displayed everything from a simple flower or happy face to deep-seated political views.

Indira Gandhi became the Prime Minister of India, serving from January 1966 to March 1977 and again from January 1980 until her assassination in October 1984.

The Beatles first performed before a U.S. audience on the Ed Sullivan Show in February 1964. Roughly three-fourths of the total audience in America - 75 million viewers tuned in to watch and hear the Fab Four sing "All My Loving", "Till There Was You" and "She Loves You". The broadcast ended with the group singing "I Saw Her Standing There" and "I Want to Hold Your Hand."

Andy Warhol rocked the art world in 1961 when he exhibited his works at the New York department store Bonwit Teller. The show helped launch his career and placed him in the forefront of the Avant-Garde art movement in the United States.

Mary Quant, a British fashion designer of the swinging sixties, started a fashion craze with the miniskirt, hotpants and colored tights.

In 1963, H.R. Ball, while working for a Massachusetts ad agency, came up with the Smiley Face image for one of their clients as a way to soothe their employees. He was paid $45 for the drawing, which he never trademarked. Since then, the Smiley Face has appeared on millions of items including a U.S. postage stamp.

The Hanna-Barbera classic, The Flintstones, debuted September 30th, 1960 and became an immediate hit.

2001: A Space Odyssey, directed by Stanley Kubrick; written by Kubrick and science fiction great, Arthur C. Clarke, came to theaters in 1968. It received tepid reviews at the time but was eventually acclaimed by many critics as one of the best films ever made.

ARPANET, the predecessor of the Internet, relayed its first communications on 21 November 1969. The messages were sent between UCLA and Stanford.

Known at the time simply as the *World Championship Game* between the best teams in the AFL and the NFL, the first Super Bowl kicked off on January 15th 1967 with the Green Bay Packers playing the Kansas City Chiefs. The Packers beat the Chiefs by a score of 35 to 10. The average price for a ticket to see the game was $12 and there were 32,000 empty seats at the Los Angeles Memorial Coliseum where the game was held.

The 25th Amendment to the U.S. Constitution setting out the steps to be taken when a president or vice president dies or becomes incapacitated or disabled was passed by Congress on July 6, 1965 and ratified by the states on February 10, 1967.

Lawyer and civil rights activist, Thurgood Marshall was appointed to the Supreme Court on August 30, 1967, becoming the first African-American to serve in the highest court.

In 1965, by an Act of Parliament, the United Kingdom abolished the death penalty.

The USSR was ahead in the space race in the 50s and 60s until 1969, when Neil Armstrong and Buzz Aldrin were landed on the moon and returned safely back to earth. Televisions across the United States and the world were tuned in to see the spectacular event when Neil Armstrong uttered the famous words, " That's one small step for man, one giant leap for mankind ".

The Ford Motor Company began production of the now iconic Ford Mustang in 1964.

Woodstock, possibly the most famous music festival of all time, took place on Max Yasgur's Dairy farm in New York from August 15th to 19th, 1969. The "3 Days of Music and Peace" attracted over 400,000 and featured thirty-two of the biggest name music acts of the time, including:

Janis Joplin, Jimi Hendrix, Jefferson Airplane, Richie Havens, Joe Cocker, and The Who.

Sesame Street debuted on American television in November 1967. This groundbreaking children's show is still on television to this day.

Originally created in the mid-nineteenth century, the Ouija board was thought to be a conduit to communicating with the dead. In the 1920s, it gained the reputation for being a dangerous game that could drive people insane. However, this "mystifying oracle" made such a fantastic comeback in the 1960s that it outsold the hugely popular game of Monopoly in 1967.

Fashion styles of the 60s included bouffant hair styles, bell bottoms of all patterns and colors, go-go boots, peasant blouses, love beads, tie dye shorts, platform shoes, mood rings, miniskirts, and granny glasses.

Bravo Smokes were nicotine-free cigarettes made out of cured lettuce leaves. They were invented by the chemist Puzant Torigian, who, after he also tested kale, grape, cabbage, kohlrabi, spinach, carrot, peanut, tomato leaves, and sugar beet tops, determined that lettuce leaves were the best tobacco substitute. Bravo Smokes went on the market in 1965, but received such consistently bad reviews for their taste (worse than smoking coffee grounds in newspaper) they had to be taken off the market. Oddly enough, Bravo "Full Flavor" cigarettes are back on the market and can be purchased online. I wonder if they still have their signature coffee ground taste?

Television goes "Where No Man Has Gone Before" when the Star Trek television series hits the airwaves in 1966.

Chubby Checker made The Peppermint Twist popular when he appeared on American Bandstand in the early 1960s. The dance was featured in films in the early sixties but quickly faded when other dances such as the Mashed Potato and the Watusi were introduced to TV shows and movies.

The Phillips Co. of the Netherlands invented the first compact audio cassette on March 5, 1962.

1960's Inventions

The halogen lamp

Valium

Nondairy creamer

The Audio cassette

Spacewar video game

Silicone breast implants

Acrylic paint

Astroturf

Soft contact lenses

The compact disk

Handheld calculator

Computer mouse

Electronic fuel injection

BASIC computer language

The artificial heart

Can You Name These 1960s Celebrities?

Answers to the Celebrity Quiz

(Left to right and top to bottom)

Barbara Feldon
Bob Dylan
Don Adams
Eva Gabor
George Burns
Gina Lollobrigida
Jack Lemon
Jerry Lewis
Jimi Hendrix
Joan Baez
Julie Andrews
Lee Marvin
Michael Caine
Omar Sharif
Paul Newman
Peter Sellers
Sandra Dee
Shirley MacLaine

Fast Facts
1960

World Population: 3,034,949,748

Bits of News

John F. Kennedy wins U.S. presidential election

Soviet missile shoots down Francis Gary Powers over Russia

Nazi murderer Adolph Eichmann captured in Argentina

3,500 U.S. soldiers are sent to Vietnam

Eisenhower signs *Civil Rights Act* into law

Construction of Aswan Dam begins

OPEC (Organization of Petroleum Exporting Countries) is formed

Echo 1, the first communication satellite, is launched

Tiros 1, the first weather satellite, is launched

Nobel Prize awarded to discovery of acquired immunological tolerance

Celebrity Births 1960

Jane Lynch (Actress)

Bono (Rock Singer)

Hugh Grant (Actor)

Antonio Banderas (Actor)

Colin Firth (Actor)

Tim Cook (CEO Apple Inc.)

Julianne Moore (Actress)

Jennifer Gray (Actress)

Kathy Griffin (Comedian)

Prince Andrew (Royal)

Valerie Bertinelli (Actress)

Sean Penn (Actor)

Stanley Tucci (Actor)

Damon Wayans (Comedian)

James Spader (Actor)

Celebrity Deaths 1960

Clark Gable (Actor)

Albert Camus (Writer)

Ward Bond (Actor)

John D. Rockefeller Jr. (Businessman)

Margaret Sullivan (Actress)

Eddie Cochran (Musician)

Oscar Hammerstein II (Lyricist)

Johnny Horton (Singer, Songwriter)

Melvin Purvis (FBI Agent)

Boris Pasternak (Poet, Novelist)

Emily Post (Writer)

Mack Sennett (Actor)

Red Byron (Race Car Driver)

John P. Marquand (Writer – Mr. Moto Spy Stories)

Leonard Warren (Opera Singer)

Academy Awards 1960

Best Movie – Ben-Hur
Best Director – William Wyler
Best Actress – Simone Signoret
Best Actor – Charlton Heston

Fiction Bestsellers 1960

Advise and Consent by Allen Drury
Hawaii by James A. Michener
The Leopard by Giuseppe di Lampedusa
The Chapman Report by Irving Wallace
Ourselves to Know by John O'Hara
The Constant Image by Marcia Davenport
The Lovely Ambition by Mary Ellen Chase
The Listener by Taylor Caldwell
Trustee from the Toolroom by Nevil Shute
Sermons and Soda-Water by John O'Hara

Tony Awards 1960

Best Play – A Raisin in the Sun
Best Musical – Fiorello / The Sound of Music
Best Actor (Play) – Melvyn Douglas
Best Actress (Play) – Anne Bancroft
Best Actor (Musical) – Jackie Gleason
Best Actress (Musical) – Mary Martin

Fast Facts
1961

World Population: 3,091,843,507

Bits of News

U.S. breaks diplomatic relations with Cuba

East Germany erects Berlin Wall

CIA attempts overthrow of Cuba –in *Bay of Pigs* fiasco

World Wide Fund for Nature (WWF) started

Yuri Gagarin becomes first human in space

IBM introduces the *Selectric* typewriter

Sweden's Dag Hammarskjold wins Nobel Peace Prize

Alan Shepherd becomes first American in space

President Kennedy asks Congress for money to put a man on the moon

Song of the Year: *Theme from Exodus*

Celebrity Births 1961

Barack Obama (U.S. President)

Princess Diana (Princess)

Ralph Macchio (Actor)

Eddie Murphy (Actor)

George Clooney (Actor)

Billy Ray Cyrus (Country Singer)

George Lopez (Comedian)

Wayne Gretzky (Hockey Player)

Michael J. Fox (Actor)

Randy Jackson (Pop Singer)

Woody Harrelson (Actor)

Meg Ryan (Actress)

Nadia Comaneci (Gymnast)

Isiah Thomas (Basketball Player)

Lea Thompson (Actress)

Celebrity Deaths 1961

Ernest Hemingway (Writer)

Gary Cooper (Actor)

Ty Cobb (Baseball Player)

Marion Davies (Actress)

Chico Marx (Comedian, Actor)

Dashiell Hammett (Writer)

Sam Rayburn (Politician)

James Thurber (Cartoonist, Author, Playwright)

Grandma Moses (Painter, illustrator)

Dag Hammarskjold (Secretary-General of U.N.)

Edith Wilson (First Lady)

Barry Fitzgerald (Actor)

Anna May Wong (Actress)

Lee de Forest (Father of Radio, Inventor)

George S. Kaufman (Writer)

Academy Awards 1961

Best Movie – The Apartment
Best Director – Billy Wilder
Best Actress – Elizabeth Taylor
Best Actor – Burt Lancaster

Fiction Bestsellers 1961

The Agony and the Ecstasy by Irving Stone
Franny and Zooey by J.D. Salinger
To Kill a Mockingbird by Harper Lee
Mila 18 by Leon Uris
The Carpetbaggers by Harold Robbins
Tropic of Cancer by Henry Miller
Winnie Ille Pu by Alexander Lenard
Daughter of Silence by Morris West
The Edge of Sadness by Edwin O'Connor
The Winter of Our Discontent by John Steinbeck

Tony Awards 1961

Best Play – Becket
Best Musical – Bye, Bye Birdie
Best Actor (Play) – Zero Mostel
Best Actress (Play) – Joan Plowright
Best Actor (Musical) – Richard Burton
Best Actress (Musical) – Elizabeth Seal

Fast Facts
1962

World Population: 3,150,420,795

Bits of News

Cuban Missile Crisis

Telstar commercial communications satellite is launched

Lt. Col. John Glenn Jr. becomes first American to orbit the earth

Marilyn Monroe serenades President Kennedy on his birthday

Seattle's famous Space Needle observation tower is completed

Albert Sabin develops oral Polio vaccine

Marilyn Monroe found dead od sleeping pill overdose

The Beatles are turned down by Decca Records

James Meredith becomes first African-American student to enroll in the University of Mississippi

Celebrity Births 1962

Tom Cruise (Actor)

Steve Irwin (Australian Zookeeper)

Jim Carrell (Actor)

Demi Moore (Actress)

Tommy Lee (Drummer)

Jon Bon Jovi (Rock Singer)

Garth Brooks (Country Singer)

Jodie Foster (Actress)

Jerry Rice (Football Player)

Emilio Estevez (Actor)

Bo Jackson (Baseball Player)

Matthew Broderick (Actor)

Wesley Snipes (Actor)

Sheryl Crow (Pop Singer)

Suzanne Collins (Author)

Celebrity Deaths 1962

Marilyn Monroe (Actress)

Eleanor Roosevelt (First Lady)

Lucky Luciano (Gangster)

Niels Bohr (Physicist)

William Faulkner (Writer)

Charles Laughton (Actor)

E.E. Cummings (Poet)

Hermann Hesse (Writer)

Ernie Kovaks (Actor, Comedian)

Fritz Kreisler (Violinist)

Franz Kline (Painter)

Mickey Cochrane (Baseball Player)

Rosalie Edge (Women's Rights Activist, Environmentalist)

Kirsten Flagstad (Opera Singer)

A.E. Douglass (Astronomer)

Academy Awards 1962

Best Movie – West Side Story
Best Director – Robert Wise & Jerome Robbins
Best Actress – Sophia Loren
Best Actor – Maximillian Schell

Fiction Bestsellers 1962

Ship of Fools by Katherine Anne Porter
Dearly Beloved by Anne Morrow Lindbergh
A Shade of Difference by Allen Drury
Youngblood Hawk by Herman Wouk
Franny and Zooey by J.D. Salinger
Fail-Safe by Eugene Burdick and Harvey
Wheeler
Seven Days in May by Fletcher Knebel and
Charles W. Bailey II
The Prize by Irving Wallace
The Agony and the Ecstasy by Irving Stone
The Reivers by William Faulkner

Tony Awards 1962

Best Play – A Man for All Seasons
Best Musical – How to Succeed in Business
Without Really Trying
Best Actor (Play) – Paul Scofield
Best Actress (Play) – Margaret Leighton
Best Actor (Musical) – Robert Morse
Best Actress (Musical) – Anna Marie Alberghetti
/ Diahann Carroll

Fast Facts
1963

World Population: 3,211,001,009

Bits of News

Civil Rights "March on Washington" by 200,000

Martin Luther King delivers "I Have a Dream Speech"

President John F. Kennedy shot in Dallas, Texas

British Secretary of War John Profuma resigns

Washington and Moscow "hot line" opens to reduce risk of war

Album of the Year: *The First Family*, Vaughn Meader

Beatles release "I Want to Hold Your Hand" and *Beatlemania* begins

Alcatraz federal penitentiary, known as *The Rock* closes

Korea returns to civilian rule

Kenya gains independence from Britain

Celebrity Births 1963

Michael Jordan (Basketball Player)

Brad Pitt (Actor)

Whitney Houston (R & B Singer)

John Stamos (Actor)

Lisa Kudrow (Actress)

George Michael (Pop Singer)

Mike Myers (Actor)

Conan O'Brien (TV Show Host)

Quentin Tarantino (Director)

Charles Barkley (Basketball Player)

Rob Schneider (Actor)

Jet Li (Actor)

Tom Cavanagh (Actor)

Phoebe Cates (Actress)

Vanessa Williams (Actress)

Celebrity Deaths 1963

John F. Kennedy (U.S. President)

Sylvia Plath (Writer)

W.E.B. Du Bois (Civil Rights Activist)

C.S. Lewis (Writer)

Robert Frost (Poet)

Patsy Cline (Singer)

Lee Harvey Oswald (Assassin)

Edith Piaf (Singer)

Aldous Huxley (Writer)

Medgar Evers (Civil Rights Activist)

Ernie Davis (Football Player)

Pope John XXIII (Pope)

Dick Powell (Actor)

Dinah Washington (Singer)

Adolphe Menjou (Actor)

Academy Awards 1963

Best Movie – Lawrence of Arabia
Best Director – David Lean
Best Actress – Anne Bancroft
Best Actor – Gregory Peck

Fiction Bestsellers 1963

The Shoes of the Fisherman by Morris L. West
The Group by Mary McCarthy
Raise High the Roof Beam, Carpenters, and
Seymour-An Introduction by J.D. Salinger
Caravans by James A. Michener
Elizabeth Appleton by John O'Hara
Grandmother and the Priests by Taylor Caldwell
City of Night by John Rechy
The Glass-Blowers by Daphne du Maurier
The Sand Pebbles by Richard McKenna
The Battle of the Villa Fiority by Rumer Godden

Tony Awards 1963

Best Play – Who's Afraid of Virginia Woolf?
Best Musical – A Funny Thing Happened on the
Way to the Forum
Best Actor (Play) – Arthur Hill
Best Actress (Play) – Uta Hagen
Best Actor (Musical) – Zero Mostel
Best Actress (Musical) – Vivien Leigh

Fast Facts
1964

World Population: 3,273,978,338
Bits of News

Nelson Mandela sentenced to life imprisonment in South Africa

In the U.S.S.R. Khrushchev is deposed

China detonates its first atomic bomb

U.S. Surgeon General affirms cigarette smoking can cause cancer

Nobel Prize awarded for developing the principle of producing high-intensity radiation

Dr. Martin Luther King, Jr receives Nobel Peace Prize

The Civil Rights Act of 1964 is signed into law by President Lyndon B. Johnson

Jack Ruby is convicted of murdering Lee Harvey Oswald (who assassinated President Kennedy)

The *Boston Strangler*, Albert DeSalvo is captured

Celebrity Births 1964

Jeff Bezos (Entrepreneur)

Michelle Obama (First Lady)

Boris Johnson (British Prime Minister)

Courteney Cox (Actress)

Keanu Reeves (Actor)

Sandra Bullock (Actress)

Kamala Harris (Vice President)

Rob Lowe (Actor)

Nicolas Cage (Actor)

Matt Dillon (Actor)

Bobby Flay (Chef)

Russell Crowe (Actor)

Marisa Tomei (Actress)

Sarah Palin (Politician)

Stephen Colbert (TV Show Host)

Celebrity Deaths 1964

Sam Cooke (Singer)

Douglas MacArthur (U.S. General)

Herbert Hoover (U.S. President)

Ian Fleming (Author of James Bond series)

Cole Porter (Composer, Songwriter)

Alan Ladd (Actor, Producer)

Peter Lorre (Actor)

Alvin York (Decorated U.S. Army soldier of WWI

Rachel Carson (Marine Biologist)

Jawaharlal Nehru (First Prime Minister of India)

Harpo Marx (Comedian, Actor, Musician)

Jim Reeves (Singer, Songwriter)

Gracie Allen (Comedian)

Eddie Cantor (Comedian)

Paul of Greece (King)

Academy Awards 1964

Best Movie – Tom Jones
Best Director – Tony Richardson
Best Actress – Patricia Neal
Best Actor – Sidney Poitier

Fiction Bestsellers 1964

The Spy Who Came in from the Cold by John Le Carre
Candy by Terry Southern and Mason Hoffenberg
Herzog by Saul Bellow
Armageddon by Leon Uris
The Man by Irving Wallace
The Rector of Justin by Louis Auchincloss
The Martyred by Richard E. Kim
You Only Live Twice by Ian Fleming
This Rough Magic by Mary Stewart
Convention by Fletcher Knebel and Charles W. Bailey II

Tony Awards 1964

Best Play – Luther

Best Musical – Hello, Dolly!

Best Actor (Play) – Alec Guinness

Best Actress (Play) – Sandy Dennis

Best Actor (Musical) – Bert Lahr

Best Actress (Musical) – Carol Channing

Fast Facts
1965

World Population: 3,339,583,597

Bits of News

Rhodesia declares independence from Britain

Dr. Martin Luther King, Jr. and 2,600 others arrested in Selma, Alabama

Black-Nationalist leader, Malcolm X assassinated

Race riots in Watts section of Los Angeles for 6 days leaves 34 dead, 1,000 injured and 4,000 arrested.

UNICEF (United Nations Children's Fund) receives Nobel Peace Price

President Lyndon Johnson announces program to create Medicare and expand war on poverty.

Daytime soap opera "Days of our Lives" debuts

Voting Right Act guaranteeing African Americans the right to vote becomes law

The first U.S. combat troops arrive in Vietnam

Celebrity Births 1965

Brooke Shields (Actress)

Dr. Dre (Rapper)

Robert Downey Jr. (Actor)

J.K. Rowling (Author)

Charlie Sheen (Actor)

Kevin James (Actor)

Ben Stiller (Actor)

Sarah Jessica Parker (Actress)

Shania Twain (Country Singer)

Viola Davis (Actress)

Stee Kerr (Basketball Coach)

Elizabeth Hurley (Actress)

Owe Hart (Wrestler)

Diane Lane (Actress)

Scottie Pippen (Basketball Player)

Celebrity Deaths 1965

Malcolm X (Civil Rights Activist)

Winston Churchill (Prime Minister)

Nat King Cole (Singer, Jazz Pianist)

Stan Laurel (Comic Actor)

Dorothy Dandridge (Actress)

Shirley Jackson (Writer)

T.S. Eliot (Poet)

Albert Schweitzer (Physician, Humanitarian)

Clara Bow (Actress)

William Maugham (Novelist, Playwright)

Linda Darnell (Actress)

Edward R. Murrow (Journalist)

Judy Holliday (Actress)

Dorothy Kilgallen (Journalist)

David O. Selznick (Film Producer, Screenwriter)

Academy Awards 1965

Best Movie – My Fair Lady
Best Director – George Cukor
Best Actress – Julie Andrews
Best Actor – Rex Harrison

Fiction Bestsellers 1965

The Source by James A. Michener
Up the Down Staircase by Bel Kaufman
Herzog by Saul Bellow
The Looking Glass War by John Le Carre
The Green Berets by Robin Moore
Those Who Love by Irving Stone
The Man with the Golden Gun by Ian Fleming
Hotel by Arthur Hailey
The Ambassador by Morris West
Don't Stop the Carnival by Herman Wouk

Tony Awards 1965

Best Play – The Subject of Roses
Best Musical – Fiddler on the Roof
Best Actor (Play) – Walter Matthau
Best Actress (Play) – Irene Worth
Best Actor (Musical) – Zero Mostel
Best Actress (Musical) – Liza Minnelli

Fast Facts
1966

World Population: 3,407,922,630

Bits of News

France withdraws its forces from NATO

Medicare begins in the United States

The "Miranda Act" protecting the rights of the accused decided by the Supreme Court.

The first episode of "Star Trek" is broadcast.

Insulin is first synthesized in Chine

Francis Rous win Nobel Prize in Science for discovery of tumor-producing viruses

"The Pill" is declared safe for human use

Anti-Vietnam-War protests grow, with more marches and demonstrations

The U.S. Department of Transportation is formed

The mini-skirt fad begins.

"Batman" television show premieres

Celebrity Births 1966

Adam Sandler (Actor)

Gordon Ramsay (Chef)

Janet Jackson (Pop Singer)

Mike Tyson (Boxer)

Patrick Dempsey (Actor)

David Schwimmer (Actor)

Halle Berry (Actress)

Cindy Crawford (Model)

Salma Hayek (Actress)

David Cameron (Politician)

Paul Hollywood (Chef)

Kevin de Leon (Politician)

Rainn Wilson (Actor)

Helena Bonham Carter (Actress)

Jon Favreau (Actor)

Celebrity Deaths 1966

Walt Disney (Animation Entertainment Pioneer)

Buster Keaton (Comedian, Actor, Filmmaker)

Montgomery Clift (Actor)

Lenny Bruce (Comedian)

Margaret Sanger (Birth Control Activist)

William Frawley (Actor)

Chester W. Nimitz (U.S. Navy Fleet Admiral)

Ed Wynn (Actor)

Eric Fleming (Actor)

Hedda Hopper (Gossip Columnist)

Evelyn Waugh (Writer)

Elizabeth Arden (Cosmetologist)

C.S. Forster (Novelist)

Bud Powell (Pianist, Jazz Musician)

Gertrude Berg (Actress)

Academy Awards 1966

Best Movie – The Sound of Music
Best Director – Robert Wise
Best Actress – Julie Christie
Best Actor – Lee Marvin

Fiction Bestsellers 1966

Valley of the Dolls by Jacqueline Susann
The Adventurers by Harold Robbins
The Secret of Santa Vittoria by Robert Crichton
Capable of Honor by Allen Drury
The Double Image by Helen MacInnes
The Fixer by Bernard Malamud
Tell No Man by Adela Rogers St. Johns
Tai-Pan by James Clavell
The Embezzler by Louis Auchincloss
All in the Family by Edwin O'Connor

Tony Awards 1966

Best Play – Marat/Sade
Best Musical – Man of La Mancha
Best Actor (Play) – Hal Holbrook
Best Actress (Play) – Rosemary Harris
Best Actor (Musical) – Richard Kiley
Best Actress (Musical) – Angela Lansbury

Fast Facts
1967

World Population: 3,478,769,962

Bits of News

USSR and US propose a nuclear proliferation treaty

Elvis Presley and Priscilla Beaulieu are married in Las Vegas

South African surgeons perform world's first human heart transplant

Six Day War between Israel and Arab forces

Corporation for Public Broadcasting is created

Ralph Nader's book, "Unsafe at any Speed" puts pressure on government and auto industry to improve car safety

National Transportation Safety Board is created

Supreme Court rules that bans on interracial marriage are unconstitutional

Expo 67 is held in Montreal, Canada

Celebrity Births 1967

Kurt Cobain (Rock Singer)

Vin Diesel (Actor)

Matt LeBlanc (Actor)

Will Ferrell (Actor)

Julia Roberts (Actress)

Jamie Foxx (Actor)

Jimmy Kimmel (TV Show Host)

Nicole Kidman (Actress)

Laura Graham (Actress)

Keith Urban (Country Singer)

Vanilla Ice (Rapper)

Anderson Cooper (TV Show Host)

Macy Gray (Soul Singer)

Leslie Jones (Comedian)

Laura Dern (Actress)

Celebrity Deaths 1967

Che Guevara (Revolutionary)

Jayne Mansfield (Actress)

Otis Redding (Singer, Songwriter)

Vivien Leigh (Actress)

Langston Hughes (Poet)

J. Robert Oppenheimer (Physicist)

John Coltrane (Saxophonist)

Gus Grissom (Astronaut)

Spencer Tracy (Actor)

Woody Guthrie (Singer, Songwriter)

Harold Holt (Prime Minister of Australia)

Basil Rathbone (Actor)

Dorothy Parker (Poet, Writer, Critic, Satirist)

Claude Rains (Actor)

Brian Epstein (Talent Manager)

Academy Awards 1967

Best Movie – A Man for All Seasons
Best Director – Fred Zinnemann
Best Actress – Elizabeth Taylor
Best Actor – Paul Scofield

Fiction Bestsellers 1967

The Arrangement by Elia Kazan
The Confessions of Nat Turner by William
Styron
The Chosen by Chaim Potok
Topaz by Leon Uris
Christy by Catherine Marshall
The Eighth Day by Thornton Wilder
Rosemary's Baby by Ira Levin
The Plot by Irving Wallace
The Gabriel Hounds by Mary Stewart
The Exhibitionist by Henry Sutton

Tony Awards 1967

Best Play – The Homecoming
Best Musical – Cabaret
Best Actor (Play) – Paul Rogers
Best Actress (Play) – Beryl Reid
Best Actor (Musical) – Robert Preston
Best Actress (Musical) – Barbara Harris

Fast Facts
1968

World Population: 3,551,599,127

Bits of News

North Korea seizes U.S. Navy Ship Pueblo

Martin Luther King, Jr. is assassinated

Senator Robert Kennedy is assassinated

Apollo 8 astronauts are the first men to orbit the moon

The Soviet Union invades Czechoslovakia

The Intel corporation is created by Gordon Moore and Robert Noyce

The Redwood National Park is created in California to protect the Giant Redwoods

James Earl Ray is sentenced to 99 years for the assassination of Martin Luther King, Jr.

CBS Prime -time news magazine show "60 Minutes" airs for the first time

Petroleum is discovered in Alaska

Celebrity Births 1968

Hugh Jackman (Actor)

Celine Dion (Pop Singer)

Will Smith (Actor)

Guy Fieri (Chef)

Owen Wilson (Actor)

Lisa Marie Presley (Pop singer)

LL Cool J (Rapper)

Daniel Craig (Actor)

Helen McCrory (Actress)

Kristin Chenoweth (Actress)

Lucy Liu (Actress)

Josh Brolin (Actor)

Gillian Anderson (Actress)

Phill Lewis (Actor)

Scott Morrison (Politician)

Celebrity Deaths 1968

Martin Luther King Jr. (Civil Rights Activist)

Helen Keller (Author, First Deaf-Blind Person to Earn a B.A. Degree)

Robert F. Kennedy (U.S. Senator)

Yuri Gagarin (Cosmonaut)

John Steinbeck (Writer)

Enid Blyton (Children's Writer)

Frankie Lymon (Singer)

Upton Sinclair (Writer)

Tallulah Bankhead (Actress)

Bea Benaderet (Actress)

Dan Duryea (Actor)

Marion Lorne (Actress)

Dorothy Gish (Actress)

Edna Ferber (Playwright, novelist, screenwriter)

Charles Munch (Conductor)

Academy Awards 1968

Best Movie – In the Heat of the Night
Best Director – Mike Nichols
Best Actress – Katherine Hepburn
Best Actor – Rod Steiger

Fiction Bestsellers 1968

Airport by Arthur Hailey
Couples by John Updike
The Salzburg Connection by Helen MacInnes
A Small Town in Germany by John le Carré
Testimony of Two Men by Taylor Caldwell
Preserve and Protect by Allen Drury
Myra Breckinridge by Gore Vidal
Vanished by Fletcher Knebel
Christy by Catherine Marshall
The Tower of Babel by Morris L. West

Tony Awards 1968

Best Play – Rosencrantz and Guildenstern Are Dead

Best Musical – Hallelujah, Baby!

Best Actor (Play) – Martin Balsam

Best Actress (Play) – Zoe Caldwell

Best Actor (Musical) – Robert Goulet

Best Actress (Musical) – Patricia Routledge / Leslie Uggams

Fast Facts
1969

World Population: 3,625,680,627

Bits of News

French is made equal to English throughout the Canadian national government.

The Beatles record Abbey Road, their final album together

Approximately 150,000 attend Isle of Wight Festival

Golda Meier becomes Prime Minister of Israel

Public Broadcasting System (PBS) is establishing

Senator Edward Kennedy flees the scene of a fatal accident in Chappaquiddick, Massachusetts

Stonewall riot in New York City marks the beginning of the gay rights movement

United States, U.S.S.R. and 100 0ther countries sign the nuclear Nonproliferation Treaty (NPT)

The use of DDT in residential areas is banned

Celebrity Births 1969

Jennifer Lopez (Pop Singer)

Jennifer Aniston (Actress)

Mariah Carey (Pop Singer)

Jay-Z (Rapper)

Ellen Pompeo (Actress)

Gwen Stefani (Pop Singer)

Renee Zellweger (Actress)

Paul Rudd (Actor)

Jack Black (Actor)

Matthew Perry (Actor)

Bobby Brown (R&B Singer)

Matthew McConaughey (Actor)

Marilyn Manson (Rock Singer)

Cate Blanchett (Actress)

Donnie Wahlberg

Celebrity Deaths 1969

Judy Garland (Actress, Singer)

Dwight D. Eisenhower (U.S. President)

Rocky Marciano (Boxer)

Brian Jones (Musician – The Rolling Stones)

Boris Karloff (Actor)

Jack Kerouac (Novelist, Poet)

Robert Tylor (Actor)

Jeffrey Hunter (Actor)

Howard McNear (Actor)

Thelma Ritter (Actress)

Walter Gropius (Architect)

Sonja Henie (Figure Skater)

Walter Hagen (Golfer)

Frank Loesser (Composer, Songwriter)

John Wyndham (Science Fiction Writer)

Academy Awards 1969

Best Movie – Oliver!
Best Director – Carol Reed
Best Actress – Katherine Hepburn, Barbra Streisand
Best Actor – Cliff Robertson

Fiction Bestsellers 1969

Portnoy's Complaint by Philip Roth
The Godfather by Mario Puzo
The Love Machine by Jacqueline Susann
The Inheritors by Harold Robbins
The Andromeda Strain by Michael Crichton
The Seven Minutes by Irving Wallace
Naked Came the Stranger by Penelope Ashe
The Promise by Chaim Potok
The Pretenders by Gwen Davis
The House on the Strand by Daphne du Maurier

Tony Awards 1969

Best Play – The Great White Hope
Best Musical – 1776
Best Actor (Play) – James Earl Jones
Best Actress (Play) – Julie Harris
Best Actor (Musical) – Jerry Orbach
Best Actress (Musical) – Angela Lansbury

**Thank you so much for reading this book.
I hope you enjoyed it.**

Want More Fascinating Facts?

**Get your free copy of
Now That's Interesting
by Jonny Katz**

**Please drop us an email:
OldTownPublishing@gmail.com**